PROLOUGE

Your strength is within you not outside of you, in this world we all find things that are helpful for self. Some things in our life may not be helpful for us. But it's up to everyone to accumulate the facts before proceeding with our ways and actions to bring for an understanding of who you are and not what things appear to be to someone else. Things you think, and feel are drawn from the mind. There is time to be weak and there is a time to be strong. Everyone must know when the time is right and when the time is not right. Me myself will not waste time searching for things that does not exist outside of me. Its up to Eye to master self and being able to think for self. We all at times in our life go through the hell to come out right to love it's all in how we move mathematically. This book that is based on events that have taken place in my life or someone else life and may be helpful for others. There are many people that suffer from child abuse, mental, sexual abuse and verbal abuse. Many people act different to situations. Some people may come out strong and some will come out weak. We all have a choice in life. If you can uplift someone else do so. Many people are afraid of venting to others, because of the way one may react. That's why it's very important to have people that are in your circle that are positive and that are for the betterment of self and others. One thing that is alarming that many black children are suffering in silence due to lack of support within their home and community. It takes a village to raise a child. Nowadays you have grown adults telling other people in the black community to mind their own business, until something drastic happens to one of our own. I know that many may disagree with the message I'm sending about raising our children a village. Honestly, I really think the slave syndrome stick with many of the blacks in the community and have a hard time of loving and their own people. Its not the blame games. It's the statistics and stipulation that has been label on blacks through more than four hundred years of slavery. What really sad is when you learn the truth it will be the people that look like you, that will try to tear you down and ridicule you. The truth is the truth and don't need any refinement the truth stands on its own and don't need any speakers.

EYE WAS IN THE DARK

Contents

BROKEN AGREEMENT

CHALLENGES

BIBLIOGRAPHY

Growing Up Growing up as little girl I faced hard times and many challenges within my family and growing up into adulthood. I was born in Atlanta, Georgia Fulton County at Grady Memorial Hospital on August 1,1982. My parents were Lo Byrd and Bar Byrd, I can remember as far back when I was four years old living in Atlanta Georgia. The laughter of my four brothers and one sister. My sister name was Champagne Byrd she was my mother's favorite between her and I. Being a little sister, I

like the fact that I had a big sister that I can look up to.

 My father was supposedly in the Air Force and we were a military family, so we moved around a lot across the country. My mother I don't really remember her being the happiest person, every time that I would see her, she was unhappy or aggravated to the point where she wanted to give up. My sister and I got along played together and argue amongst one another but at the end of the day I still loved her. I really can't picture my father being in my life at the time, because he was barley there and at work. I was a part of a family that had many secrets and would do any and everything to keep those secrets from coming out. As I got older and start to communicate more and more with family members that I have never me that when the strut had started to come out. One day in the wee hours in the morning my mother decided to pack up with my siblings and I and leave Atlanta to come to Cleveland Ohio, I don't remember the year nor the exact date. All I remember was being on the Greyhound and looking at all the strange people that were on the bus, my brothers were rowdy on the whole bus ride. On the way to Ohio my sister

Champagned got locked in the bathroom on Greyhound and my third oldest brother Nate was making scary noises to scare her. I though that was the funniest shit ever. The bus driver that was driving had to pull the bus over to the side of the road to unlock the bathroom door so that my sister would be able to get out. After that happen my mother told me that when one of us girls had to use the restroom on the bus, that one of us had to stand by the door. I wasn't laughing no more.

The day my family arrived to Cleveland Ohio I never thought that there were going to be trials and tribulation and hard times. As a little girl not knowing what was taken place at that time in my life with my family. I knew that I had to go through hell to come out right to love. I started school at Woodland Hills Elementary school in Cleveland Ohio. I was six years old and starting kindergarten. I can't recall at that time if my little brother Ed went to school with me or not, my memories is vivid. As a little girl I had difficulties seeing and I had to wear bifocal glasses which I was teased for wearing. At that time my mother, Lo faced a lot of hardships due to my father Bar being on drugs. At this point we were living in an apartment on 93rd and

Dickens off Kisman. My mother tried her best to be the mother that she could, at least I thought. That's when the nightmare of my life began to change and my whole world began to be turned upside down. When I was seven years old and was looking through the broken window that my brother Nate had cracked my head, when he was mad at the time at my mother. He pushed my head through the broken window inside the bedroom that me and my sister Champagne and I shared at the time. The broken glass of the window in the apartment caught my head and from falling from out the window. I screamed so loud that my mother rushed into the bedroom and seen my head and body caught inside of the window. She grabbed a bunch of

EYE WAS IN THE DARK

5

towels and wrapped them around my head while waiting for the ambulance to come and get me. During the whole commotion of everything my little brother Ed told my mother that my third oldest brother Nate had pushed me through the window while I was looking through the window. Lo then focused her attention at her third oldest son Nate, she takes her one foot while holding me with the towels still wrapped around my head and kicks him with so much force that he went into the wall falling. By the time the ambulance arrives I was rushed to the nearest emergency room. My brother Nate had to go as well because his eye was bleeding from my mother kicking him into the wall with one of her one foot while holding me. She was on fire and whooped him so much that you'll have thought that he would change for better. Things down the line for Nate only gets worse. That's another whole story. Well go figure all the damage in the apartment on Dickens off 93rd of Kisman, caused my mother to be evicted with six children. We then resided with my grandmother who name was Milly. Lo and my grandmother never seen eye to eye on nothing in life. My grandmother felt that my mother treated my sister better than she treated me gave her more attention than she gave me. Eventually; my grandmother put my mother out of her house with six children because of her ways and action. We also lived with my auntie Jackie which was my grandmother's younger sister. My aunt was the best, but again my mother and her didn't workout with living arrangements. Due to the fact that my three oldest brothers Bar Jr., Nakia, and Nate were hardheaded and didn't like being told what to do. As well my mother didn't like for no one to tell her what to do with her children. It caused her ways and actions once again to be homeless and into a shelter with six children. A few weeks down the line we moved into another home a single-family small house off East 93rd Elwell of Woodhill Avenue. That's where all the shady things taken place before being removed from the care of my mother and father. Even though my father was rarely round the family in the physical we knew he was alive, he would come over to ask my mother could he his children high on dope. She was furious and would tell him hell no you can't see your children, until you clean yourself up off drugs. My three oldest brothers at the time was bad as hell you could not tell them nothing. Anything you told them went into one ear and out the other ear. Lo would be so angry that whooping them didn't seem to help at all. One day she stops coming home and me and my little brother Ed, and older sister Champagne would look for her to walk through the door. Only to look up one day and found out that she had a new man in her life Uncle G would drop by and check on us when we came home after school, because my mother was not there to care for us. And my first oldest brother Nakia would abuse us why my mother left him in charge of us at the time when she was not home. He was the worse and would make me and my little brother and older sister hold our hands out and hit us in the hand with a thick ass wooden stick. Afterwards; he would tell us if we cry, he would hit us even harder. But when Uncle G comes over it was a wrap for my oldest brother Nakia, he tore his ass up and didn't play no games. Oh, did I mention he was my aunt Jackie husband. He brought food to the house when my mother couldn't afford to feed us and stayed with us at times to make sure we were safe. One morning I woke up and got dressed for school as usual and my brother Nate would walk me, Ed, and Champagne to school every morning. I was then seven at that time and was going on eight years old that year and was attending Buckeye Woodland Elementary. However; I was permitted to catch the bus home after school. The school bus would drop me off in front of my door steps. But one day I was trying to get in my house and the door was locked and the driver told me to get back on the bus. As I heard the bus driver talking to the dispatched from the bus radio, I was then taken to Family and Children's Services. At that moment I thought that my mother did not care about me at all. One of the Social Workers had told me that my mother had moved back with my grandmother Milly and that's where all the other five children were. I was hurt and sadden by all the things that

were taken place in my life at that moment. With no knowledge on the moved and I was told nothing on the day of morning I left out and went to school. It was a white male middle aged Cleveland police officer that had taken me to my grandmother's house where my mother resided back once again with her mother. There were times she would leave us in the wee hours of morning and go see her new boyfriend that she was dating going on year. Not knowing down years from now that the two of the Jesse and my mother would get married. As well be locked up years later for murder. One morning while I was at school and was in class, the principle at Buckeye Woodland pulled my teacher Ms. Boris from that classroom and was chatting with her. After they were finish, I was then told to gather my things and go with the principle which whom name I could never remember. All I remember was that she was a white woman. When I got to the principal's office my little brother Ed was sitting in the office and my oldest and only sister Champagne was sitting in the office as well. We were told to sit there and that someone was coming to get us. All I can remember from that day was a black middle-aged woman and a white man name Marino came and sat down and started talking with us. That's when we realized that they both from the Department of Children and Family Services and we were being put into an institution until they could find foster care for all three of us. The institution we were put in for children of all ages was a placed called Metzenbaum Center, there were four units for all different aged children two Units for little girls and big girls, two units for little boys and big boys. I had just turned eight years old that following year.

The System

Being in the system was not the place to be in especially being away from your family and not being able to see them. It's something that would having you feeling detach away from the world, feeling. Emotionally disturbed. At Metzenbaum Center my little brother Ed was placed in the little boy's unit, my sister Champagne and I were placed in the little girls' unit. But before me and my sister were taken to Metzenbaum we were placed far on the west side of Cleveland Ohio in a foster home old back lady looking like she was in her mid-60s. She was mean as hell and hit my sister with a cane for stealing food out the refrigerator. Afterwards; sister called the kids hotline and we ran away, well tried. We were caught and then placed at Metzenbaum where we placed with my brother.

In the units at Metzenbaum my sister and I barley spoke with other little girls that were in the unit and for the first few days we kept to our self. My little brother eventually found a way to talk to us through the plugs in the game room whenever we got the chance to go in the game room. My three oldest brother Nate, Nakia, and Barron were placed in a group home called Jones home. They system figured since they were teenagers at the time that they could spend the rest of their time aging through the system.

In Metzenbaum you had to follow the rules and obey orders that were given by the staff inside of the units. There were days I was so suicidal that I didn't even bother to get out of my bed. I shared a room with three other girls and there were two bunk beds inside each of the eight rooms that were located inside of each unit.

EYE WAS IN THE DARK

7

There was also a big dining hall where all the little girls and the little boys ate together in the dinner area. I guess you can say it's almost like a prison. Truth be told an institution is a prison where a person does not have their freedom to go as they please and is looked over twenty-four hours of the day. It was hard getting used to being around people I didn't know, but o had no control over my life at eight years old. I was now a ward of the state and paid dearly mentally and physically.

There was a game room down stairs in the
Metzenbaum and when people were well
behaved, they earned at chance to be in the
game room. It was this one little girl name
Arron that didn't like me for no reason, she was
about the same age as me. She was a bully and
thought that she can pick on people smaller
than her. At the age of eight I did not know how
to fight; my brothers fought my battles for me
before I was taken from the care of my mother
Lorain. One day while we were down in the
game room, I got tired of Arron's bullying and
decided to take up for others and myself. While
she was putting her hands on a little girl and the
girl started crying while everyone else in the
game room looked on. I put down the Nintendo
remote that I held in my hand and started
attacking her. While she thought she was
getting the best of me. I took her by the hair
and slammed her head down on the edge of the
table leg in the game room. One of the staff
members came and restrained me. I was taken
up stairs and taken back to my unit and stripped
of all privileges of any playing or game room
time. However; I did get the chance to go to
regular schools.

The school at the time I attended was McKinley Elementary on the westside of Cleveland and was in the third grade. I was being bullied in my class there as well. I was so angry at all things that had taken place in my life that I had built up anger and resentment towards everyone in my life. I fought everyone that thought that they could put their hands on me and not be taught life lessons of bullying. I was kicked out of school afterwards. At Metzenbaum so much abuse of me and other children had taken place that I was removed to a new institution called Beech Brook. Beech Brook was located in the middle-class section on the east side of Ohio, surrounded by nothing but woods.

Beech Brook

Being on the grounds of Beech Brook were very different from Metzenbaum. Beech Brook has cottages and the boys and the girls were not separated and they also had a school located on the grounds. The cottage I was in was called Austin cottage. The children and I had our group meetings in the cottages and as well went to school on grounds as well. The name of the school was called Gund. We did majority of our activities there on the grounds we rarely went off grounds to do anything or take trips. When the parents came to visit, we had a hall to spend one one time with our parents. The two years I was at Beech Brook I can only remember my mother to come and see once or twice. My dad he never visits around that time, he was on a vacation in prison for a few years.

While I was on the grounds of Beech Brook I had a therapist at the time that I was seeing her name was Ann Sylvester. She would ask me questions about my childhood as a little girl when I lived with my mother. However; she had the notes to the truth of my background. I really felt as a little girl at nine I really didn't care about anything. I had no empathy for no one in my life during the time of my life.

At the age of ten I moved into a new home by a woman name Isha she was a good mother to her two daughters, even though I felt ignored and not a part of her family. Being a foster child in someone else's home is not heartwarming. But she did have a challenge with me dealing with my emotions and mental capacity to get along with others at home and abroad. One day while I was living with her my mother called and we spoke for a minute. The next thing I know

her and my foster mother Isha were arguing
never knew what the argument was about.
After that day a worker cane and got me from
Isha house and took me to live with my aunt
Jackie one of my mother's aunt who was also
my great aunt. The thing that had bother me
the most was that my mother didn't have her
shit together. It was like a hit in the head like
you lied on my foster mother Isha to social
worker. And my thing was regardless of the
situation I felt as though my mother made my
life complicated by lying and knowing that she
did not want any parts of me. The day I arrives
to aunt Jackie how all I had to bring with me
was a pillow and two bags of clothes. At that
time, I was eleven years old. I got enrolled into
a new elementary school called Mt. Pleasant
which I graduated from. Then I went to junior
high at Alexander Hamilton which I was kicked
out of school from brining a knife to school.
After I got jumped by three girls it was over, I
played no games no more afterward. In the
school and the streets, I earned a named for
myself called Madmax. Which I thought the
name fitted me because if my anger anger, I
always fighting not taking no shit. Before
getting kicked out of Alexander Hamilton a riot
had started on the second-floor lunchroom and
was told it was my fault. However; the girl

jumped up in my face throwing her hands up and talking about what o want to do. So, I punch her in the face and start swing throwing jabs until she hit the floor. By the way that girl name was Carla. The Cleveland Municipal school district decided that I should finish my seventh-grade year at home with offsite tutor which I did. I was expelled went to Juvenile and was put on probation. Afterwards; I was sent to a school for bad children, which was called Green View. Green View went from K-12. I actually met my goals there and was sent back to the public school in the tenth grade.

The Cleveland Public High school I attended was called South High school. I was a Muslim and wore my hijab and stayed dressed in 3/4. It was hard times back then for me to adjust back to regular school. I tried my best to stay out of trouble. Somehow; it wasn't that easy I started being teased about my glasses so I started fighting. One day I cut school and had a change of clothes so I would go this girl house I was cool with name Becca. After changing my clothes, I would leave and meet up with my soon to be child father name Demont. I met Demont while I was skipping school and went to Tower City in downtown Cleveland and he asked me what my name was and I told him Max was my name Me being the girl that I am naive not knowing who this man was at all we would go over his mothers house and that's how my first child Riq got here. You would really think that some things in life were just that simple. It was not that simple to me yet the hard as what, not knowing what the next day was going to be like.

Pregnant One day in the summertime my aunt Jackie had taken me on a family reunion where we went to Alabama and we were at the mall shopping she had noticed that I couldn't get into the dress she wanted me to try on for a ball that the family was having. The dress was too small and I couldn't fit into it. My aunt then said "hey girl you know that you been gaining a lot of weight, I hope that you are not pregnant". I know what I have done and have not told her about a guy name Demont. Eventually I would have to tell her and I did just that shortly after we have arrived back to Ohio. Afterwards; she was hot and was questioning me on how I was going to raise a baby when she had to work. Aunt Jackie then took it upon herself to schedule my

EYE WAS IN THE DARK

9

appointments for prenatal care for me and the baby. I would be by self and asking questions for self and learn on my own. I didn't know how to be a mother of another human being. All I knew was I had to give my unborn child a better future than I endured. Once my son was here, I was going to be a better mother than my mother and not let my child suffer at the hands of other, regardless to whom or what. Being pregnant with my first child made me feel a little depressed, of course I had my Aunt. But the one person I wanted in life around this time was my mother Lorain. Being a ward of the state was drastic and being pregnant. I did not question the things that went on in my life growing up. I just knew from experience that there were good and bad people. That means that at the time I got pregnant with my first child at the age of fifteen by a grown man was wrong. I knew that cutting school was wrong as well too. However; the situation was already born into existence and there was nothing that I could do to change the situation that I created on my own. There were times living with any aunt that she would try and talk to me, it just went in one ear and out the other. All I knew was that I had to take care of my unborn son once he was in the physical of this world. This world that has so much hate, envy, jealousy, and lust that at times it becomes mind blowing. I was never perfect so I did not care how people viewed me, because I knew a difference from religious people and nonreligion people. There are many challenges that as a mother that I knew that I was going to face in the end when it came down to having my son. In which I thought that was one of the best things that ever happen to me Even though that I was not prepared of what to come into play in my life by having a son. I went to all my appointments and follow ups with the doctor for my prenatal care while I was pregnant. I had stop talking to the father of my unborn child at the time. Besides being fifteen and messing with a man that was seven years older than me, my aunt would have wanted to press charges. Being so young and not taught how to act at home and abroad, my life was in shambles. I would also lie to my aunt and not reveal the truth of who the real father at of my unborn child. I told her that it was my friend Ali who house I would go over every time that I got angry at my aunt. The lie became so bad that Ali's own mother thought that the baby was his and he knew that the baby was not his. I think we both thought that it was quite funny to lie and make everyone think that he was the father. I learned later down the line that lying about the father of my child did not make me look good as a woman. It made others that were around me look at me differently it would take me years to change. Becoming the woman that I wanted to become. Because of the childhood and the things that I gone through in my life it was hard. The reason was that I became bitter and angry about the things that I have been through. And with change of life it starts with me Divine. Becoming a mother was unbearable going to school and having to focus on the things in my home circumference was becoming unattainable. Aunt Jackie house was being renovated so I had to either be homeless or stay with other relatives. In which I did both became homeless and stayed with relatives while pregnant and still going to school. My unborn child would arrive three weeks early due to my stress and toxemia. I was transferred from the clinic to the Metro Health hospital where I was taken to the Labor and Delivery unit to have my labor induced. When my son arrived into this world, CDFS came and tried to take my son away from me on the strength that I was still in the system. My aunt Jackie step in and sign the papers for me to keep my son. I named my son Riq. He would be the one who would change my life forever and becoming a better person in life. Anyone can give birth to a child, but not everyone can be a mother. A mother is the child first teacher and nurse. That means that if you are ignorant that means that you are illiterate and are unable to teach your child anything.

Mother Role One would think that being a mother would be an easy task at hand. After giving birth to Riq I moved upstairs in my aunt house with mu cousin Rell. She was one of them quiet low key keeps to herself type of people and didn't do too much talking. One of the things that I loved most about my cousin Rell was she was a good example of being a good mother and how to keep to your own damn self. It would take me the hard to learn that. I was so depressed at times that I thought that I needed friends. The only friend that I needed in my life was self. Riq was a hand full a March son and a spoiled one on top of it. I would let him cry and still try and get sleep and my cousin Rell would give me that look. That look that I'll beat your ass if you don't get that baby and stop him from crying. I'll eventually pick him up hold him and cry silently with him while patting him on the back to stop crying. Having a child so young made me feel like a failure in life. I couldn't do the things that I wanted to, now that Riq was here he went everywhere with me. His appointments I never missed nor he ever wanted for diapers and milk. Financially my aunt Jackie help out and it didn't surprise me. Because at the age of 11 years old she taken me into her home. Three months passed since the birth of Riq and I really felt that my mother should meet my son her first and only grandchild at the time. I then went to have a conversation with my aunt about my mother, explained my feelings about her. My aunt knew how my mother felt about me and treated me before she lost her custodial rights. However; I felt that if I moved back in with my mother that Riq would bring joy to her life. I would eventually make that moved and saying good bye to my aunt Jackie's house. The arrival to my mother's house felt good and I felt at home again with my siblings. We were older and I was 17 my older four siblings aged through the system and only three of them moved backed with my mother before I arrived. Ed my little brother was still in foster care, would come over my mother's house and visit on the weekends. Ed and I were close and we had a bond that no one could no break regardless to whom or what. After moving in with my mother our bond was still the same, we were not close and her love for me was not there either. She loved Riq and would watch my son while I was still trying to finish high school. One day out of the blue she told me that she was not watching my son anymore. While Riq was 6 months old I started taking him to school with me. The high school I attended was East Tech and I was in the 12th grade and daycare was inside the school. So everyday I went to school so did Riq. It was coming close to graduation and I had to meet with the guidance counselor about graduation. I was told that I had to pay senior dues and go to night classes in order for me to graduate. Unfortunately; me finish high school had to go on hold. I got into too many fights and got kicked out. It would take me a year later to finish high school and walk across the stage to graduate. No one in my family attended my graduation. But I was all too happy that my son's father Demont would join my ceremony with our nine-month-old son Riq siting there applauding. Now that I completed high school, I felt like I was on top of the world. My next step was college and to obtain employment to take care of my son. I felt that moving back with my mother was the biggest mistake that I made in life. And that reason was she thought so small of me and was the one that said "that I would not finish high school". It was almost that she my own biological mother didn't want to see me succeed in life. I made a promise to myself that I would never treat my child or any of my future children the way she treated me. It was as if she hated the sight of me and anything that I did good for her or myself it was not satisfying to her at all. Living in my mother's house with an infant was not the business and I should not have been in her house hold at all, with all the negative things that was going on. Being in mother's house was hell and I was for one was not going to keep staying around for the bullshit. In life we all have choice rather they are good or bad you will receive a reward and that's the law of the universe. The choices that I made while living with my mother would damn near cost me my life and

EYE WAS IN THE DARK

11

losing my son to the system. After moving in with my mother she was taking my checks from Social Security and was only giving me enough to take care of my son. While my sister Champagne and my second oldest brother live with mother for free and didn't have to pay shit. I felt some type of way and was angry and start to resent my whole family for the way I was being treated. When I had to go and take care business, I would take my son everywhere I went. The damn daycares couldn't trust them either almost went to jail for them letting my son bust his head open, where he need stiches. I was one of them people that I was so angry that I fought and really didn't care at the time going to jail. Now writing this story I really was being selfish with the decisions that I made in life. I got myself into a bind with the Feds, I met a guy name Dred who showed me how to make good quick money. I didn't have to sell my body nor drugs. It was checks and the first time I was nervous, after that it was a breeze. Not realizing what my consequences were going to be, I was going to pay. I felt that the situation with my family was all screwed up. I fell on hard times that I had to do what I needed to do to make ends meet and take care of Riq and myself. During the struggle a lot was changing before my eyes not knowing what was to come next. I started dealing with high explosives. I met a guy name Nickel in 2003 and not knowing his true intentions, I would become pregnant a second time with another son. When I gave birth to baby Nickel me and my relationship got worse than ever. Baby Nickel had gotten sick at two months old where he had to be hospitalized at

University for two weeks. During baby Nickel two weeks in the hospital the staff gave us our own room where me and Riq would stay the night. I went to school and took Riq to daycare. Afterwards; it was back to the hospital with baby Nickel. At this time, me and big Nickel had broken up because I couldn't deal with a guy that was going to cheat on me with one of my friends and then lie to my face. He still was a father to his son even though we were not together. My mother she did not care for him that much she thought the worse of him. But damn I hate to say it she was right and my judgment was wrong. When baby Nickel was three months old my mother put me out of her house with my two sons in the cold October of 2004. As a mother I had to think of the well being of my children and could not let them suffer as I did in the system. So, I did the only thing that I thought was good for my children. I called big Nickel on my cell phone and explain the events that just unfolded between my mother and I. I explain to him that he had to get his son fast and that my mother called the police on me and put me out with my two sons. He was man enough to come and get threemonth-old Nickel and Riq was four around this time he would stay with me. I felt that my life was spiraling out of control. All the money that I got from busting the checks with Dred, I gave my mother some of that money. And she had the audacity to put me out of her home because I checked my sister from putting her hands on Riq. I told my sister Champagne that I would bust her ass messing with mine. Of course, as usual my mother took her side and decided that I was not welcome in her home any longer. I thought to myself that I should of listen to my aunt Jackie's words of wisdom "you can't make someone love who don't love you or themselves". She was right, it took me to find out the hard way for myself. Life at the time was becoming more and more complicated that I fell into a state of deep depression. At the point where I taken a knife and slit my left wrist crying and feeling like no one in this world cared for me. It hurts growing up with parents that don't love you and would just let the state come and grab you from the only home you knew. And put you in an institution with about two hundred other children. I was lit and very angry at the world and also blame myself for many of the things that happen to me in the system. My mother knew that I was being abused and violated. It's like she didn't care and that my word was not valued. Big Nickel and I made an oral agreement that he would take care of baby Nickel until I got myself together.

Riq and I went to go and live with a friend of mine name Just. Just open his home to us and

welcome us in his home. A few months later that situation would become a disaster. Just started to put his hand on me and inflict verbal abuse on me. Riq he loved him as if he was his own child, again I was putting my own needs before my children. I took it upon myself to get a job and the only job that I got was working at McDonalds in Tower City downtown Cleveland. It was cool and the work schedule was perfect for my Riq and I during this time. His school was just right up the street a half of mile. I grew tired of Just having to take care of me and then thought I owed him a favor. Just never called me by name Divine (Maddy) he always uses derogatory language towards me. I understood that Just had lost his father recently in the year of 2003, it still did not give him the right to take all his frustration an anger out one me. One of the biggest lessons I learn in life from being with Just was, never date someone that you were friends with. Just beat me so bad in 2005 that I went to work at McDonald's with a bruise on my face and swollen. I did not care what people thought of me, I still had to make my money. They say pay back is a bitch and pay back is what I did to Just. After this man beat me like I was a man I tried to burn his house down and took some pills. Oh, before I did that, I beat up his Caucasian girlfriend. Next; it was time for murder suicide. Riq was in school when the events were unfolding. The only thing that I knew is that I woke up in a mental psych ward at St. Vincent and Charity hospital where I had to stay for a few days. While I was in the psych hospital the daycare lady name Mary kept Riq for me the whole time. She didn't mind she did daycare from home and she was the only person during this time I trusted. While I was in the psych ward, I called my aunt Jackie and letting her know everything that I was going through and needed to come back a live with her so that Riq and I get our lives together. The one thing she wanted to know is why I didn't call her when the incident taken place between my mother and I. She said "I told you what was going to happen before you moved back in with your mother Divine (Maddy)". She let me make my own decision so that I would learn for myself the way my mother felt about me. Before leaving the hospital at St. Vincent Charity they wanted to make sure that I had services set up for counseling and a stable home for Riq. While I was living with Just, I did get a chance to see baby Nickel. Over the couple of years big Nickel having baby Nickel he would soon change up on me and having lawyers call my job trying to get custody of baby Nickel. Trying to get me to sign my right over to him. Big Nickel didn't realize that he was dealing with a fighter and I was not going to let him have my son. We had an oral agreement and he broke that agreement. I grew hate for him.

Broken Agreement

In the year of April 2005, I lost my grandmother on my mother side Mally. She would always have my back when my mother and I got into disagreement. I felt like someone had taken my world when my grandmother went back to the essences. This was still around the same time that I was getting out of the abusive relationship with Just, and big Nickel breaking his oral agreement with me. I didn't know if I was coming up or down it was just so much that was going on at one time and I was win college. In which I would then decide to change my major from private investigation and start going for criminal justice. However; at this point in my life I was not sure what I wanted to do or how to handle the things that were currently taking place with me and my two children. I knew that Riq was good, but baby Nickel I was not to sure about. Big Nickel had broken his oral agreement between him and I. He felt like he had the power because he had my baby boy. I was making too many moves at one time and not realizing that one step at a time, then I'll been fine. I moved back in with my aunt Jackie that year of 2005. I gave up fight for baby Nickel around this time until I gotten my shit together. I had now the realize the reason why county step in and taking me away from my mother. She was not making the best choices for her children to preserve the best part for us. That made

EYE WAS IN THE DARK

13

me look in the mirror at who I was and what type of life that I wanted to offer my children in the near future. I had to build a solid foundation for my children to stand on so that they would be stable. Without no foundation you have nothing but stagnation. Stagnation is when everything stops and there's no progress. In 2006, my aunt Jack decided that she no longer wanted the house she was living in, and decided to move in the suburbs. It was time for me Maddy (Eye Divine) to handle her business and do what she needed to do for herself and family. That was when I had my Uncle G to take me too look for a place to live that year and I did. It was a one bedroom for me and Riq enough room for the both of us. I would give him the room and make the living room my bedroom. I also had a patio. The house had no furniture nor a stove. I got the apartment for a deal that I fix up the house without happen to pay a deposit. It was just me and Riq and still working at McDonalds was cool I worked full time a still kept the same schedule. I decided to start going back to school and would see baby Nickel every two weeks and that was the deal at the time between Big Nickel and I. He was still upset about me not signing over my rights to him so he still felt some type of way. He was so unhappy with me, that he went and told his family members that I was only giving him fifty dollars for my son. Which it didn't bother me because I knew the truth and the few people that were around me at the time knew the truth as well. At the end of the year when I filed my taxes from working, he would get a thousand dollars from me, and that's when he would let me see baby Nickel. I think that he was kind of mad at the fact that I had my own place and didn't need him for shit. In the year of 2008, I met a man name San he would be that one that put that smile back on my face and make me love again. I took my time with him, because I didn't want to rush into anything. I felt that was my downfall and reason that my relationships in the past didn't work. I was rushing in too fast and when you give your all it makes one look messy. I felt good about the things that were going on in my life. Until my mother called me and said "it was two Caucasian men that came to the house looking for me and, on the cards, they left it said secret service". I already knew why they were looking for me and I dint even bother to go over to her house to get the cards them devils left. I said to myself if they wanted me so bad that they knew where to find me. Come one now they are Feds secret service and can find anyone they want too. One day I was coming home from work and seen the Feds sitting outside of my home and I didn't run I kept acting normal and went inside my home. One of my family friends who name was Man told me "I'm going home because you did some shit that I don't want no parts of". I said "that's fine Riq don't need you to watch him because I'm here and he can start going to daycare after school". In the late fall of the year of 2008 I was indicted for fraud and other chumped up charges. I guess them devils thought I was supposed to sing like a canary not me. I felt if you have your evidence then you don't need me to further your investigation. It was not about trying to save anyone ass. Dred would not do the same for me. The reason was that man disappeared when I got indicted, I was by self to take the fall. And I damn sure was not going to listen to all these fake street lawyers who thought that they knew the law. When I knew one thing for sure that I was not going to let them devils know shit. Get your criminals like you so claim gotten evidence on me. I knew that the constitution did not protect the rights of blacks in America. I also knew that we didn't have any freedom, justice, nor equality in the wilderness of North America. Another charged that the Feds was trying to pin on me was conspiracy against the United States. When I seen that crap in the indictment papers I started laughing. Trying to feed my family was one thing, but honestly that charge had me thrown way aback and mind bottle for a minute. In 2009 I was pregnant with my third son Chez, by San. The whole time that I was pregnant with Chez I was going back and forth to court. The only people that had my back at the time was not blood related. So nowadays it does not bother me who is in my corner or not, it always me against this wicked ass people in this world. Eventually; after all the court proceeding, I left the federal court building feeling lovely. I had a pro bono attorney Joe that represented me in my federal case. I was giving restitution, three years probations, and mandatory therapy. I think that my background saved my ass from going federal prison. However; I still was angry at the fact that I had a charge of uttering checks it was my first felony and only and there was no leniency. That's how I felt and still to this day. If I was a Caucasian male or female, they would have just given me a tap on the shoulder.

Challenges

Life became difficult for me as mother after receiving the news of my second son father being killed in a car accident on his way to a funeral. Nickel came to live back with me after the death of his father Nickel Sr. I was not aware of the challenges I had to face with young Nickel after I got him back. Transitioning as I knew for Nickel in my home was not going to be easy. I had three other children as well. Riq who was the oldest, Chase who was the third born and Lana who was my daughter the baby out of all four of them. Nickel has issues in the school that he currently attended at the time upon his arrival in my home. He attended Miles Park Elementary the teacher and principal would call my phone three times a week or more. I grew agitated with the phone calls about Nickel behavior. So, I started just to sit in the classroom with him and at times do pop up visits. That was working for a minute. However; one day while I was at work, I got a call from the security guard from Miles Park Elementary telling me that my son was in the hospital, at University Hospital. When I rushed to the hospital, I found out that my son was trying to commit suicide and that they would be keeping him for evaluation due to his young age. I had my oldest son Riq attend to the other children while I was at the hospital with Nickel. Deep down inside I felt bad for my son and felt that I should never have him to his father at three months old. However; it was too late to point any fingers I had to what was best for my son and be the mother I needed to be and not become like my mother Lo. There are people that go through things different from others and handle things different from others. My back was against the wall as a young mother of four children. My children didn't ask to be born into this world, they came through me and it was my duty to be their teacher and guide. Nickel stayed in the hospital for a week for psych evaluation and I was there every step of the way. Upon his release from the hospital I had to put in footwork take him to psychiatric appointments which was kind of far from home. So eventually I decided to set my own doctors up for Michael I even had a counselor to come out to the home for him to readjust back to reality. As I seen he was having a hard time over the death of his father. My life as mom would be difficult and hurtful in the end with Nickel.

There were happy days and there were bad days, some days were harder than others. I still went to work and stayed being a mother. At this point my relationship with Chase and Lana father started to take toll for the worse after being together for six years it was wrap. It was too much tension between us and Nickel as well. I chose my son happiness over my own. Which at the time I though my happiness didn't even matter? All I wanted to do was make sure that all my children were good. I could not deal with the little one's father discipline of my children and his infidelities. It was a time for me to step my foot up a notch and be a mother to the fullest. It was hard but after being single it felt that life was becoming easy and simple. I also switch Nickel school and put him in E Prep

Elementary. At this time change need to be done and changes I was making for all four my children. Riq was not too much of a problem and Chase and Lana we still babies.

EYE WAS IN THE DARK

15

When changing Nickel school, I thought I was doing a good thing I knew that transition for him was going to be difficult. Nickel now seven decided he wants to keep using his father death as a way of acting out and start telling lies on people. So, I decided to seek help for my self-dealing with one son that has mental issues. I knew in my heart and mind that this was going to be a difficult journey for Eye. I stayed being loving to my children I stayed on top of the things as a mother. I would learn later in life that one child that you would give everything up for would hate you the most out of all your children just that one. Nickel kept having these temper tantrums and making irrational decisions. I really felt that he hated me for giving him up to his father. However;

Nickel didn't realize that I was gave him to his father so he would not be homeless or put in the system. I guess he couldn't understand what events taken place over the years he would grow hate for me. Nickel kept doing whatever he thought he could do and get away with it as well and I wasn't having it. One day while going up to E Prep Nickel was being restrained by a staff at the school. When he seen my face, he utters the word "I hate you bitch". I told the staff to let him go so I can whoop his ass. She saying "you can't put your hands on him in here at school". I look at that chick crazy like you restraining my son though. I was hurt so bad I cried hearing those words coming out of my son mouth. It would not be the last time I hear them words from Nickel either. Nickel had an Individual Educational Plan (IEP) put in place for his behavior and mental issues as well put into a special class. Somehow change was going to be harder than I thought for Nickel. E Prep grew tired of Nickel so they decided to expel him and send him to a new school in the suburb for special children. The new school Nickel would attend would be called ELA. In the state of Ohio, it is kind a hard to raise your child in a systematic racism system. When trying to go and get help for Nickel it all landed back on me and the behavior would eventually grow increasingly worse over the years to come. Giving this child all my love and attention just seems as it wasn't good enough for him. I wasn't sure what it was, all I could think about was it must be me or the other children. Nickel wanted life to be his way regardless of matter at hand at the time. The older he got the more challenging it became for me to raise him and difficult for me to leave the little ones with him because I didn't trust him. Riq was older he was helping as much as he could. Riq eventually got shot at the age of 15 hanging with the wrong people who he thought was his friend. He grew tired of the issues in the house and Nickel so at the age of 19 Riq decided to move out on his own. Nickel blame me and everyone else for a Riq leaving home and not himself. Every time there was an issue Nickel would say "why blame everything on me, I'm always the one getting into trouble and no one else". However; it was Nickel that was starting all the trouble in the house. He felt as if I start trouble in the house, he would be able to go over his play sister house Nisha. Nisha was Nickel's Sr. step daughter from an ex he was dating and knew at the time. Nickel little knew her since she was a baby so they were close. I also had informed Nickel that I didn't have to let him go over his play sister house all because he was acting out just so he could get out of the house. My patience for this child started to grow really thin and my nerves were becoming more agitated. There just some shit I was not going to keep taking from my second eldest son Nickel who thought that he can say and do whatever he wanted and if I punished. He would make me pay by attacking the little ones and he would eventually go to school with a few bruises. In the end I still had to be a mother to him and my other children. At the same time, I could not keep letting my little suffer and become harm mentally or physically by Nickel. I let him know that I brought you in this world and I can take you out. It's funny how the system want help much with your child until they do something of breaking their laws. This society is a set up for black male child all over the globe.

When guiding my children and teaching them I always let my children know I am that mother that would be there by your side. But you have to make sure that you are right and not in the wrong. I also let them know as well that when they are in the wrong, they should never want me or anyone else to be by their side. That's total devilishment and I'm not teaching my children that way. If other parents want to raise their children up to do wrong to others that's fine. I'm different and cut from a different cloth. Everyone is entitled to their own persona. It's sad that children want to be like those of their peers that are hard to lead in the right direction. I let my all my children know when I give you the knowledge of who you are and you don't accept it don't blame me for when things go wrong in life. I also let it be known as mother I never really beg for shit, I got off my but and did for myself. Nickel would turn out to be the greatest and hardest lesson for me as a mother. Love was just not enough for Nickel and he didn't want anyone else having the attention but him. Rather it was man, woman, or child. I decided to let him know as a child thing don't work the way you always want them to be. He ignored my example and what I said. Nickel would come home and would always compare himself to other children situation, he attended school with. The sad part is that love and teaching him was not good enough. I was told by some people that were older than me that some children will be that one child that would give you the hardest time out of any of your other children. They were right. Doing what right by any child is the right things to do. But there's nowhere in a parent manual to tell you how to be a mother or rear your child. My children can have the world. I reward good behavior for my children's ways and actions. There were times when some people felt that as I was hard on my children and it will be caused them to go astray an unrighteousness lifestyle. You can give all that you have, in this wicked society your children are looking at others in there surrounding. I been in system and knew how it was in the streets as a child. That was something that I was not going to let my children go through. I stayed hard in my children teaching them the knowledge of self. However; I knew what my children were learning at home, that they were not going to get that type of education in the institutionalize school. Where they on teach the black children American history and not their history. I was taught each one teaches one teach one. You give a person a cup of water but you can't make them drink it. That was Nickel I gave him the cup of water, but he refuses to drink the water which I handed it to him. In addition; Nickel thought that I was going to suffer mentally. Sometimes your children will grow up and will become other than self. At some point in life that child has to accept responsibility for their own way of life, they have chosen. Especially after Nickel was giving good orderly direction. My son will learn that he will suffer in his own inquiry and his blood will not be on my hands.

He will be beat with many stripes. I take charge
of accountability of the things I have done as a
mother. However; I think that my son resent me
for giving him to his father when I became
homeless. As a woman I did what I knew best
that was for Nickel a three-month-old child, and
his father was right there. Being homeless was
hard having to get my shit together, I never did
any drugs or prostitution. I kept my oldest son
Riq and got my shit together. Elevating One
must look in the mirror at their own self in
order to change self. Self-realization meaning
that no one can love you better than self and
that's fact over everything. In this world you will
learn that the one must come before the two
and the things that people say you can't take on
face value. As a mother you can give your
children only what you know and what you
were taught. However; when you lead your
children in the right direction and they continue
to go left. Don't blame self for that child's
decision making in their adolescent age. Some
people always want to blame the parents for
the failure of that one child, not realizing that
parent was educated and self-taught on truth.
There are times many will say well how you
know the truth. Well the truth doesn't have no
speakers and it stands on it own. Mathematics
is the key to life of unlocking all the lies that you

were told. Taking the one through nine and adding back to zero. You must start from zero to get one and then

EYE WAS IN THE DARK

17

all the way through nine. A person has to be willing to change and accept the things that they have been through in order to move on. After you know the truth, you can't blame no one for the mistakes that you make in life. Everyone is indifferent just as the universe is indifferent. Elevating means learning from the past and starting a new future for self. One must have a firm foundation to build on, if not you don't have nothing to build. If you not building you are only destroying. Build means to add on to the things that are positive and destroy is taking away. Either you going to add on to your circumference for the betterment of self, or you taking away for the bad. You can also destroy things when they are not good and healthy for your life. When you have the mindset that you are strong in this world you can become anything that you want to become and there is nothing in your way stopping you.

Many people feel that you must fall before you can get back off your feet. That may be true for some but not for all other people. Defeat one must face in order to face fears and challenges in life that you thought that you could not do in life. If you apply yourself to daily task and make it be known to self, You can born that ideal into existence. My children have shown and proven to me that I can be righteous and do right by others without the attempt of deceit. It taken me a while to learn that wisdom is your ways and actions and I have to show and prove as Eye Divine who I am on a daily bias. There's going to be people that will try and lead you in the wrong direction. It's up to self to go in the right direction and become something great. Be a mother you have good and you have bad times. Living is something hard to do, it's the legacy that I want to leave my children. With being a teacher and a leader. Also give my children the Knowledge of Self of who they are. Meaning knowing who they are and the history of their ancestors. That is something that no one can take away from them. In life we learn to move forward from the pass and change who we are before we can move forward. There are some in my past life that may hinder me from other from the career that I wanted and that was to be a lawyer and advocate for abuse women. Once you realize your potential you are able to change and create new goals in your life. Being a mother and the things that I have went through did not kill me, It only made me stronger and learn from my past mistakes and become a better person. There's not a single person in this world perfect we just have to live and learn. One must know self in order to proceed and grow in life. Elevating is growing and personal develop of health and mental. Too many people are committing suicide unable to face their problems or not having any one to vent to. That's why trust is a matter of keeping your word bond to self, before you can keep your word bonded with someone else. I personally learned that you can not trust everyone or have too many friends and that was one of the reasons why I kept to myself and enjoyed being a lone with my children. I recommend for anyone that wants to elevate and grow and develop health wise or mentally should reach out to someone that they trust and talk with them. At times when I was growing up, I would cry and hurt myself when I was alone, because fighting of the pain growing up in the system and not being able to see my parents and siblings. Still till this day I hate the system for what they have done to me putting me in the care of stranger to victimize me.

However; there was one foster home that I was in and she loved me dearly and I still reaches out to her until this day. When you elevate self, you are able to elevate others. Meaning to share empathy for what others are going through in their time of need. It is a time an age where people bury their feelings in and it's hard for them to dig them feeling out. Them are the people that needs the most help to elevate their own growth and development. The sad part of being in the system, is that I have seen so much suffering and pain where some children give up on life. Some even go to the extent of suicide or being murder. The world can make you happy or sad but the choice is up to

each individual to make. We all have choices that we must make rather the choices are good or bad. Many people fail to realize that everyone in this world is served justice due to good rewards and bad rewards, you just have to pick. Elevating is also a higher position that you can find yourself when you come out the hell of darkness into the light. To go through the hell of being miserable, you damn sure can come out right to love. That's why I was taught to do the knowledge first look, listening, and observing. That means that you are able to respect the science of all things in life and that apply that one. Many people elevate off the others doing well in life. It gives he or her a reason to reach their own goals in life and to overcome a thing that they have been through. Yes, it is true that people have their outlets of how they handle things. However; there are many people who suffer from emotional distress and not as strong as others. This is the reason why elevation is mathematical. You never know who you can change and who's life that you can aspire to become something better in their own life. As life goes in you can either elevate or stagnate. Stagnation only keeps you in your feeling and stop you dead in your tracks. It is highly imperative to be around someone who is going to be a support system in your life. Having a support system can lead to a great way success of becoming whatever you want to become in life. I know many have heard the words of becoming an over achiever. Well I look at that differently it depends on how an individual add their math to their life. Haven't you heard of mixing the wrong ingredients and your recipe turns out to be a disaster? Well that the same thing as mathematics you have to start with one before you can get to the two. It's that simple. Never let someone tell you who are and what you know. Remember make chess moves not checkers. You can connect four all you and

that's what you're going to get. Get that four
and simpler as that. Don't let anyone cause you
to defect in the Knowledge of Self. Causing you
to spin out and have divided thoughts. The devil
isn't settled on the best part of the planet Earth.
That's why the best part I preserve for myself.
Building to manifest an Understanding of Self
mentally, elevating higher. Destroying the
injustice and inequality that the devil has put
into practice causing a disturbance of peace in
the Universe. Born into existence righteousness
of truth. Thru my Wisdom you will see my
Equality. By the way I treat others equal to me
and show the same quantity of time he or her
show me. I do what a Builder do and keep
adding on elevating my mental. Destroying the
cold currents by staying in my warm currents.
There are different layers of currents he or her
be in and don't even know it. Some currents are
really cold and warm and some very swift and
changeable. Eye Divine know that water can't
get out the Earth's atmosphere with its high
speed of rotation around the Sun makes it
impossible. Earthquakes are caused by the Son
of Man experimenting with high explosive.
When shit explodes in my face. I either learn or
don't learn. I'm going to Zig Zag Zig.

EYE WAS IN THE DARK

19

Bibliography

Allah School in Mecca (Harlem, NY) - New York, New York ... www.facebook.com › Places › New York, New York

www.facebook.com › Places › New York, New York 1. Similar Dayone Smith reviewed Allah School in Mecca (Harlem, NY) — star. Allah gave us the best parts of himself when he born us into the knowledge of ourselves. From that point, he continued to add onto the best part by securing us a home within the root of civilization being Mecca (Harlem, N.Y.). Address: : 2122 Adam Clayton Powell Jr Blvd; ... Phone: (212) 665-4175

Allah School in Mecca (Harlem, NY) - Facebook
m.facebook.com › photos

m.facebook.com › photos 1. Cached Allah
School in Mecca (Harlem, NY), New York, New
York. 2.4K likes. Education.

Allah School in Mecca (Harlem, NY) on
Instagram • Photos ... www.instagram.com ›
explore › locations › allah-school-in-mecca-
harle...

www.instagram.com › explore › locations ›
allah-school-in-mecca-harle... 2235 Posts - See
Instagram photos and videos taken at 'Allah
School in Mecca (Harlem, NY)'

Carmelo Anthony Visits Allah School In Mecca -
The Source

thesource.com › 2014/07/26 › carmelo-
anthony-visits-allah-school-in...

thesource.com › 2014/07/26 › carmelo-anthony-visits-allah-school-in... 1. Cached Jul 26, 2014 - The NBA star stops by the international headquarters of the 5% Nation in Harlem yesterday. After the media and fan inquiries in April over Jay-Z ...

Five-Percent Nation - Wikipedia
en.wikipedia.org › wiki › Five-Percent_Nation

en.wikipedia.org › wiki › Five-Percent_Nation 1. Cached 2. Similar The Five-Percent Nation, sometimes referred to as the Nation of Gods and Earths (NGE/NOGE) or the Five Percenters, is a movement founded in 1964 in the Harlem section of the borough of Manhattan, New York City, by Allah the ... The New York City areas of Harlem ("Mecca") and Brooklyn ("Medina") were named after ... History · Social and political ... · Conflicts · Beliefs

Allah, the Father's assassination: 48 years later | New York ... amsterdamnews.com › news › jul › allah-fathers-assassination-48-year...

amsterdamnews.com › news › jul › allah-fathers-assassination-48-year... 1. Cached Jul 13, 2017 - Clarence 13X (Allah) the founder of the Nation of Gods and Earths Wikipedia ... the second weekend of June, the Harlem-based Five Percenters aka the ... First, at their national headquarters (the Allah School In Mecca, 2122 ...

Contact Allah School in Mecca for the details 2122... - Allah's ... fiveprercentgodsnearths.tumblr.com › post › contact-allah-school-in-...

fiveprercentgodsnearths.tumblr.com › post › contact-allah-school-in-... 1. Cached Jul 16, 2015 - Contact Allah School in Mecca for the details 2122 7th Ave Harlem, NY 10027 212-665-4175.

Allah School in Mecca (Harlem, NY) Instagram posts - Picuki ... www.picuki.com › location › allah-school-in-mecca-harlem-ny

www.picuki.com › location › allah-school-in-mecca-harlem-ny

EYE WAS IN THE DARK

21

1. Cached Explore Instagram posts by Allah School in Mecca (Harlem, NY) - Picuki.com.

CITY OF NEW YORK MANHATTAN COMMUNITY ... - NYC.gov www1.nyc.gov › pdf › Allah_Justice_and_the_Five_Percenters_Square

www1.nyc.gov › pdf › Allah_Justice_and_the_Five_Percenters_Square 1. Cached PDF Powell Jr. Boulevard to "Allah,

Justice, and the Five Percenters Square." ... New York City's Public Schools before working numerous odd jobs throughout Harlem. ... Keith Wright; the Allah School in Mecca Street Academy; Allah's School.

Allah Youth Center In Mecca - Elementary Schools - 2122 ... www.yelp.com › Education › Middle Schools & High Schools

www.yelp.com › Education › Middle Schools & High Schools Allah Youth Center In Mecca in New York, reviews by real people. Yelp is a fun and ... 2122 Adam Clayton Powell. New York, NY 10027. Harlem. Directions.